D1328747

Tony Bradman is the author of many popular children's books, and is probably best known for his stories about Dilly, the world's naughtiest dinosaur. Tony has also edited many successful short story and poetry anthologies.

Other picture poetry anthologies compiled by Tony Bradman include:
All Aboard the Toy Train
Here Come the Heebie-Jeebies
The Hairy Hamster Hunt
Off to School

Published in Great Britain in 2002 by Hodder Wayland,
an imprint of Hodder Children's Books

Editor: Katie Orchard
Inside design: Jane Hawkins

Catologuing in Publication Data
Wild and Wonderful!: Poems About the Natural World. – (Picture Poetry)
1. Animals – Juvenile poetry 2. Children's poetry, English – Pictorial works
I. Bradman, Tony, 1954–
821.9'14

ISBN: 0 7502 3929 8

Printed in Hong Kong by Wing King Tong

Hodder Children's Books, A division of Hodder Headline Limited
338 Euston Road, London NW1 3BH

Produced in association with WWF-UK.
WWF-UK registered charity number 1081247.
A company limited by guarantee number 4016725.

Wild and Wonderful

poems about the natural world

Compiled by Tony Bradman
Illustrated by Susan Wintringham

HODDER
Wayland

An imprint of Hodder Children's Books

WWF

Produced in association with WWF-UK

Animal Alphabet

A is an Ant and B is a Boar.
C is the Cat by the kitchen door.
D was the Dodo. It's with us no more.
E is an Elephant, F is a Fly,
G is a Giraffe who holds her head high.
H is a Hawk who sweeps through the sky.
I is an Ibex, whose twin horns are curled.
    So many Creatures to make up a World!

J is a Jay, black, pink, white and blue.
K is a lolloping Kangaroo.
L is a Lion you'll see in the zoo.
M is a Mole or a Mouse or a Mite.
N is a Nit (grown up it will bite).
O is an Owl that hunts in the night.
P is a Peacock with bright tail unfurled.
    So many Creatures to make up a World!

Q was a Quagga (now only in books).
R is a Rat or a family of Rooks.
S is a Shark; how dangerous he looks!
T is a Tiger. Is U Unicorn?*
V is a Vole on the edge of the corn.
W's a Wren, who can nest in a thorn.
X I don't know. In confusion I'm hurled.
      So many Creatures to make up a World!

A Yak and a Zebra on Africa's plain;
An Antelope, Bear, Cheetah, Dog (a Great Dane).
Oh, here I am starting all over again!
But please understand what I'm saying to you.
We need all the Creatures. We need them, we do.
The Flea and the Wolf and the White Cockatoo.
      And, like the poor Quagga, and like the Dodo,
      If we're not very caring, they're likely to go.

*There's no such thing really
But I still love them dearly.

Gerard Benson

A Harvest Mouse Asks...

Look at your thumb.
I'm that size.
Kids think my little black eyes
are the cutest things
they've ever seen.
But I like my tail.
It's like clever string
that helps me to climb
high in the corn
where I build my house
and nibble my seed.

Please, if you see corn
waving and free
don't tread it down
but leave it be.
I'm the harvest mouse.
Remember me.

Philip Burton

Butterfly

A wink of wings
adorned with rings
  butterfly, flutter eye.

A blink of blue,
a pearly hue,
  butterfly, shutter eye.

A darting dazzle,
a wingtip frazzle,
  butterfly, flutter eye.

A flare of flowers
above she towers,
  butterfly, shutter eye.

A coloured clasp,
a painted clasp,
  butterfly, flutter eye.

A chemical field,
a polluted river,
  butterfly, won't live forever.

John Rice

The Cool, Funky, Urban Fox

Life became very hard
When I was driven from the farmyard,
Robbed of any place to hide,
Hounded from the countryside.
So one day, without looking back,
I hit the railway track,
Headed for the city lights
To join the urbanites,
And put down my scent
In a new environment.

I established my den
In a neglected garden,
Near the bottom fence
Where the thicket is dense.
I ain't no fool,
By day I play it cool,
But by night
I rummage through rubbish bins,
Scavenge discarded tins,
And trust me,
There are scraps of leftover meat
Littering every High Street:
Burgers, Kebabs, Chicken Tikka Wings,
Spicy Beef Pizza with Onion Rings,
Spare-ribs in Barbecue Sauce and Deep-fried Fish,
Just about every dish a hungry fox could wish.

And when things get grim
And the pickings are slim,
I've been known to kill the odd grey squirrel,
Or the occasional pet –
Rabbit is my favourite.

Now that you know the score
You may think I'm rotten to the core,
But look at it from any which way,
I'm definitely here to stay!
For I'm now a cool, funky, urban fox,
Streetwise and hard as rocks,
And ready for open combat,
In my new concrete habitat.
So tell me,
Have you got a problem with that?

Errol Lloyd

More, MORE, MORE!

We need more shopping centres,
More space to park our cars.
We want fast roads to drive on,
We want more burger-bars.
We want ten million houses,
We want a big new school,
We want another airport,
  A gym and swimming-pool,
    We want a three-lane ring-road,
      We want more high-speed trains,
        And twelve-screen multiplexes
        With noise to dull our brains,
        And leisure centres, ice-rinks,
        Five hundred megastores.
      We want it and we'll get it –
Give us more and MORE and MORE!

Can anybody hear us?
We need to live here, too.
We'd like to share your planet
If that's OK with you.
We need our grassy meadows,
And woods and streams and ponds,
And tangled bits of woodland,
And moors that rise beyond.
Please leave us roadside verges,
And mud and silt and sand.
We need small holes and crannies,
And scruffy bits of land.
We'll fit around your edges,
We don't demand a lot,
Just –
       please DON'T USE THE WORLD UP –
It's the only one we've got!

Linda Newbery

Golden Lion Tamarins

Lighting up the forest
with their coats of spun gold,
these tiny little monkeys
look wise and old.

Peeping in between the leaves,
clinging with their claws,
they whisk among the branches
on their strong, agile paws.

Not so very long ago
these tamarins, so rare,
were nearly lost forever.
They needed special care.

Modern zoos took family groups
and made them special cages.
Babies followed; now we hope
they'll live on down the ages.

Lighting up the forest
with their coats of spun gold,
lion manes and slender tails,
enchanting to behold.

Penny Kent

Tiger Cub

Tiger cub, so small and new,
whatever will become of you?

Will you play down by the river,
tail a-twitch and ears a-quiver,
and learn to pounce on butterflies,
sunlight dancing in your eyes?

Will you stalk the forest floor
leaving tracks with your huge paws
as you prowl through dappled light,
camouflaged by day and night?

Will you hunt with power and grace,
muscles rippling as you race
from the shadows, leaping, bounding,
a blur of stripes with speed astounding?

Or will your beauty fade and dim,
an old, moth-eaten tiger skin,
your head a trophy on a wall,
your powdered bones a folk cure-all?

Tiger cub, it's not too late.
We can save you from that fate.

Jane Clarke

Silver Back Gorilla

Through undergrowth and the gauze nets of mosquitoes,
Solid as an all-in wrestler, the gorilla takes
His morning's slowly-waddled muscular stroll,
Shaking leaves on the lower slopes of his extinct
Volcano. The earth smells rich and mossy-damp
In his rain forest; vines and herbs scent his trail,
His track, as he eats away another day – juicy leaves,
The soggy pith of his banana trees, the sweet stringiness
Of bark. Watch him shin up trunks then slide down
Like a weightless astronaut. Hear him bark and beat
His bongo chest saying, "Keep off my grass, keep out
Of my paradise, my peace and plenty! *Go Away!*"

Matt Simpson

Orang-utan

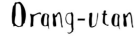

Watch me,
touch me,
catch-me-if-you-can!
I am
soundless,
swung-from-your-sight,
gone with the wind,
shiver of air,
trick-of-the-light.

Watch me,
touch me,
catch-me-if-you-dare!
I hide, I glide,
I stride through air,
shatter the day-star dappled light
over forest floor.
The world's in my grasp!
I am windsong,
sky-flier,
man-of-the-woods,
the arm of the law.

Judith Nicholls

Rapping Rhino

I'm a city boy. I was born in the zoo
I'm a streetwise kid in everything I do
Got my hide roughed up, got my horn just so
I'm a right-on, radical, rapping rhino.

So why do I dream of a place I've never been
It's a deep wet forest and it's dark and it's green
And there's no fence around it and I'm free to roam
And I don't understand it but it feels like home.

I'm a cool city kid. I strut about my pen
But I think about that forest every now and then
I ask my mum and she hits me with her snout,
"Don't pester me, boy, keep your nosey horn out!"

But I just can't do what my good mother said
'Cause the forest in my dreams keeps pounding in my head
And there's huge tasty leaves and there's high tangled vines
And it smells so good, and it feels like mine.

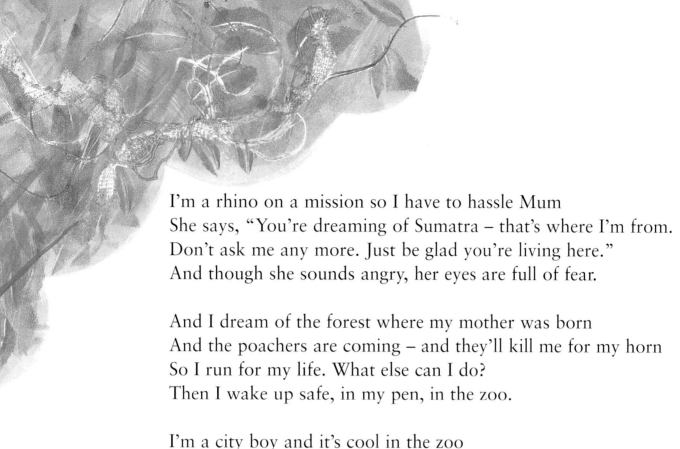

I'm a rhino on a mission so I have to hassle Mum
She says, "You're dreaming of Sumatra – that's where I'm from.
Don't ask me any more. Just be glad you're living here."
And though she sounds angry, her eyes are full of fear.

And I dream of the forest where my mother was born
And the poachers are coming – and they'll kill me for my horn
So I run for my life. What else can I do?
Then I wake up safe, in my pen, in the zoo.

I'm a city boy and it's cool in the zoo
I'm a streetwise kid in everything I do
Got my hide roughed up, got my horn just so
I'm a right-on, radical, rapping rhino.

Jan Burchett and Sara Vogler

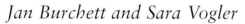

The Threatened Ark

High branches weave a roof top in the rainforest,
where a galaxy of green leaves hides a world of wildlife.
An ark
unguarded, and under siege.
Unaware,
Gibbons and spider monkeys skitter and sky-dive.
Sleepily a sloth,
moves slowly, unseen.
Crabs crawl, and tree frogs spawn in a small lake collected in the petals of
a huge flower.
Vine-like snakes slither and slide.
Brilliant butterflies
light up leaves.
Lizards leap or laze in heat
while baby parrots test their wings.
At night, a choir of Katydids makes music for the giant centipedes'
midnight feast of frogs and mice.

yet
all
the
world
seems
green
and
moist
and
still.

The forest floor is damp and dark, with fallen leaves and bits
of bark.
Here, tiny creatures live their lives, with mushrooms as their trees.

Brenda Williams

Bei-shung

I am Bei-shung, they call me the white bear.
I am the hidden king of these bamboo forests,
Invisible with my white fur and my black fur
Among this snow, these dark rocks and shadows.

I am the hidden king of these mountain heights,
Not a clown, not a toy. I do not care
To be seen. I walk, for all my weight,
Like a ghost on the soles of my black feet.

Invisible with my black fur and my white fur
I haunt the streams. I flip out little fishes;
I scoop them out of the water with my hand.
(I have a thumb, like you. I have a hand.)

Among this sparkling snow, these rocks and shadows,
I roam. Time is my own. My teeth are massive.
My jaw is a powerful grinder. I feed
On chewy bamboo, on small creatures, fish, birds.

You call me Panda. I am King Bei-shung.

Gerard Benson

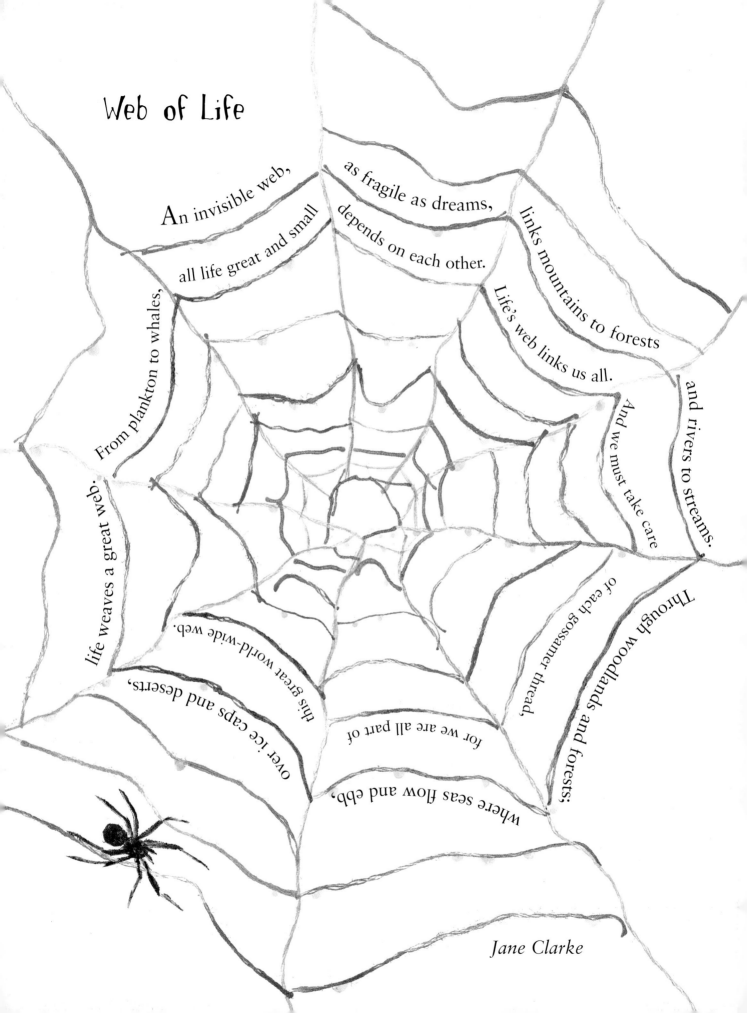

Web of Life

An invisible web,
all life great and small

as fragile as dreams,
depends on each other.

links mountains to forests

Life's web links us all.

and rivers to streams.

From plankton to whales,

And we must take care

life weaves a great web.

of each gossamer thread,

Through woodlands and forests;

over ice caps and deserts,

this great world-wide web.

for we are all part of

where seas flow and ebb,

Jane Clarke

Polar Cub

This way, that way?
Step out,
little five-toe flat-foot,
squint-eye,
cave-dazed,
into the sun!

Eyes left,
ears right,
nose to the wind!

The coast is clear!
Run, roll, lollop;
winter's done!
Enjoy the pause;
make your mark
on this blank page –
the world is yours!

Judith Nicholls
(from STORM'S EYE)

The Playful Dolphin

How good it is to wake
Among dear friends and family
And then to spend the day
Exploring wonders of our sea.

How good to feel the water's
Friendly stroke against my skin,
How good to feel that tingle
When through ships' bow-waves I fin.

How good it is to frolic,
What fun it is to play
That shadow game beneath the shafts
Of sunlight in a bay.

Be the sky dark grey or azure,
Be the surface calm or torn,
What fun it is to be alive…
How good to have been born!

Philip Waddell

Natterjacks

The small, buff-coloured natterjack
with yellow stripe along his back

comes creeping down, as evening falls,
from sand dunes to the pool. He calls

to tell the other toads he's there.
They gather in the twilight where

they croak until the air vibrates
with music to attract their mates,

as twilight grey becomes night black
with magic of the natterjack.

And if we keep the shoreline clean,
the pools, the dunes, the grass between,

this prettiest of toads will stay
to tune the night and cheer the day.

Alison Chisholm

Whale Music

Great underwater zeppelin,
sea-salt singer,
hoovering up
the soupy oceans,
the minestrone waves!

When I first heard
your thar-she-blows,
your old grampus
huffing and puffing,

I thought you were
some enormous sea-horse
snorting…

and when I saw
your tail-flukes flop
and plunge

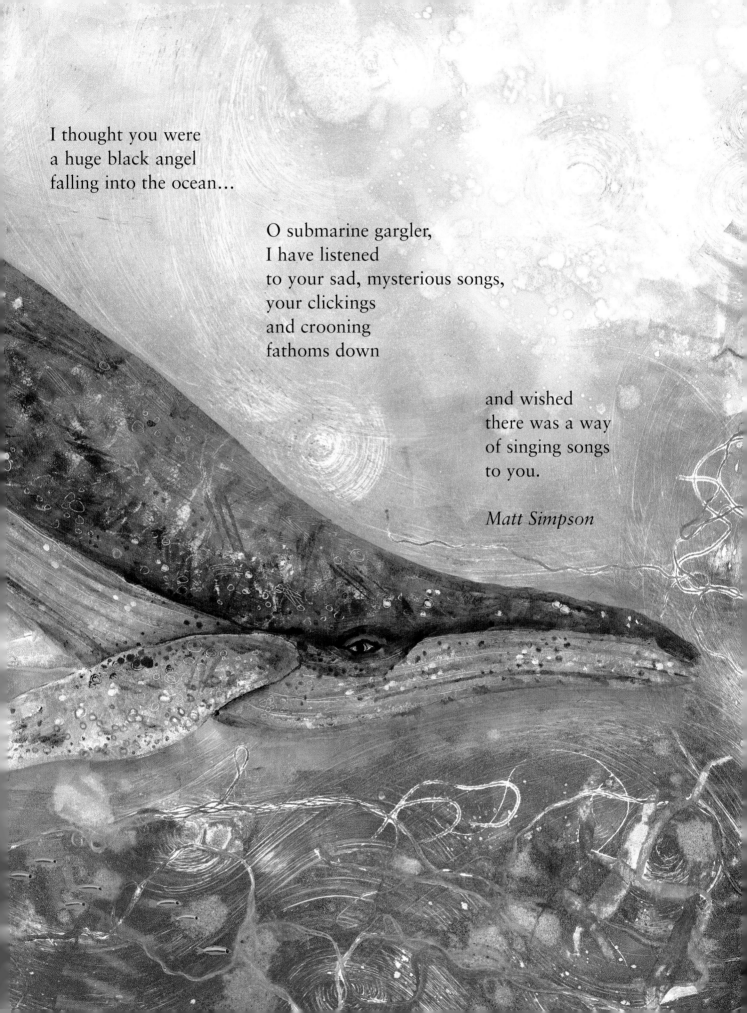

I thought you were
a huge black angel
falling into the ocean…

O submarine gargler,
I have listened
to your sad, mysterious songs,
your clickings
and crooning
fathoms down

and wished
there was a way
of singing songs
to you.

Matt Simpson

Cod

I am the queen of the ocean,
pale grey on the sandy bottom.
Stop chasing me, stop hunting me.

I am green among eel-grass,
silver by the light of the moon.
Stop chasing me, stop hunting me.

I swim on great journeys,
migrating across the open seas.
Stop chasing me, stop hunting me.

I have millions of children,
but you catch my children in nets.
Stop chasing me, stop hunting me.

I can live for twenty years,
if you will let me.
Stop chasing me, stop hunting me.

"You are the queen of the ocean,"
a fisherman told me one morning.
But where are my sisters?

I am the queen of the ocean,
red in the algal seas.
Stop chasing me, stop hunting me.

William Bedford

Loggerhead Turtles

On a balmy, quiet summer night
the cove is dim in the moon's pale light.

Small waves ripple and softly swish
over bubbling crabs and tiny fish.

Bobbing, bobbing, dark humps appear,
coming in through the water, drawing near.

Turtles! They've swum together to land
to lay their eggs in the soft warm sand.

Heavy and slow they haul up the beach
till they're far from the water's furthest reach.

Each scoops with her flippers a circular hole,
smooth and curved, a sandy bowl.

Hundreds of eggs drop, creamy and round,
into the freshly dug scrapes in the ground.

The turtles cover their eggs and go.
What will happen to them they'll never know.

Months later at night, see a wondrous sight;
the babies are hatching and taking flight,

scuttling eagerly down to the sea,
into the water, weightless and free.

Penny Kent

Lubberly

Deep under ice I am
lubberly, blubber-warm
rolling and playing

I dive, I dive
I graze icebergs,
nobody knows

but me how many
caves and chambers
an iceberg grows,

I backstroke in
then with a swoosh
I'm gone, unharmed.

Flubbery, lubberly,
blubbery, that's me.
Up on the rocks

out in the sun, how clumsy –
you watch me
flump and slither

lumber, clamber.
You think how lucky
not to be me,

but down in the deep
green rush of current
flubbery, lubberly

lucky, that's me.
Down in the deep
green rush of current

Helen Dunmore

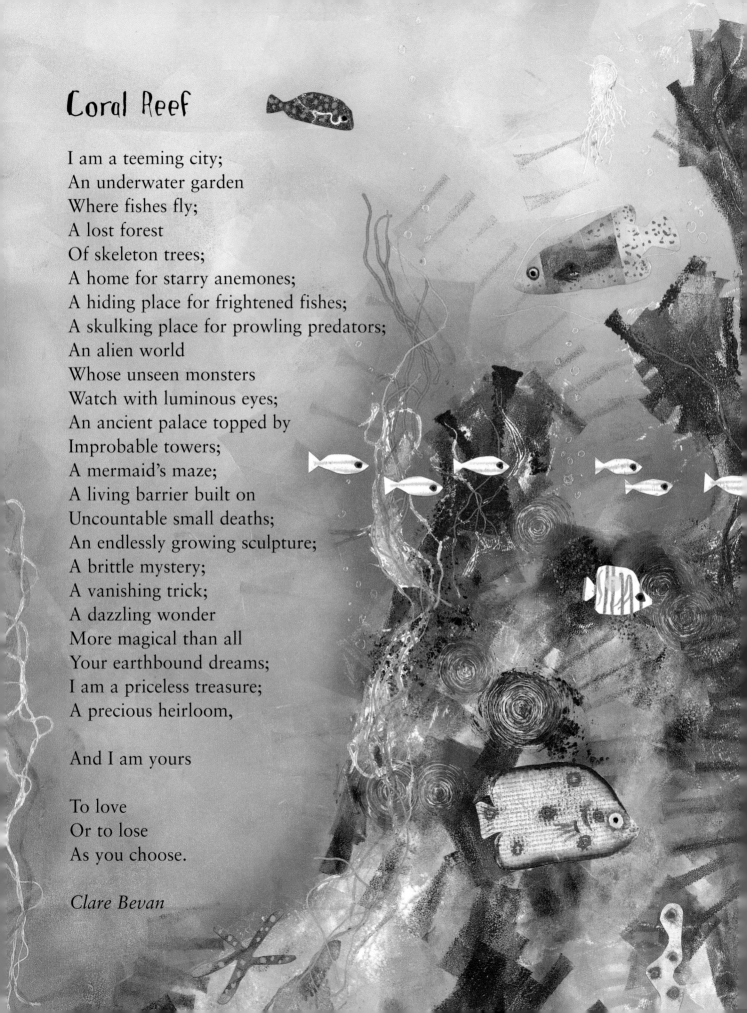

Coral Reef

I am a teeming city;
An underwater garden
Where fishes fly;
A lost forest
Of skeleton trees;
A home for starry anemones;
A hiding place for frightened fishes;
A skulking place for prowling predators;
An alien world
Whose unseen monsters
Watch with luminous eyes;
An ancient palace topped by
Improbable towers;
A mermaid's maze;
A living barrier built on
Uncountable small deaths;
An endlessly growing sculpture;
A brittle mystery;
A vanishing trick;
A dazzling wonder
More magical than all
Your earthbound dreams;
I am a priceless treasure;
A precious heirloom,

And I am yours

To love
Or to lose
As you choose.

Clare Bevan

Afterword from the WWF

(WWF-UK, Panda House, Weyside Park, Godalming, Surrey GU7 1XR)

Wild and Wonderful! celebrates the amazing richness and diversity of the natural world. It also reminds us of the part we play in the web of life and that, wherever we live and whatever we do, our actions have an impact on the natural world. When a species is in danger, it is a warning that all is not well in the environment in which it lives. Sometimes natural disasters have an effect on animal populations, but all too often, animals are put in danger because of human actions. Modern technology, increasing demands on natural resources, and the growth in human populations have put enormous pressure on fragile habitats – with disastrous consequences for many animals. It is vital that we take action now if we want to ensure a healthy planet for future generations of animals and people. Discovering more about the wondrous variety of life, and appreciating it in art and poetry, is a step on that journey.

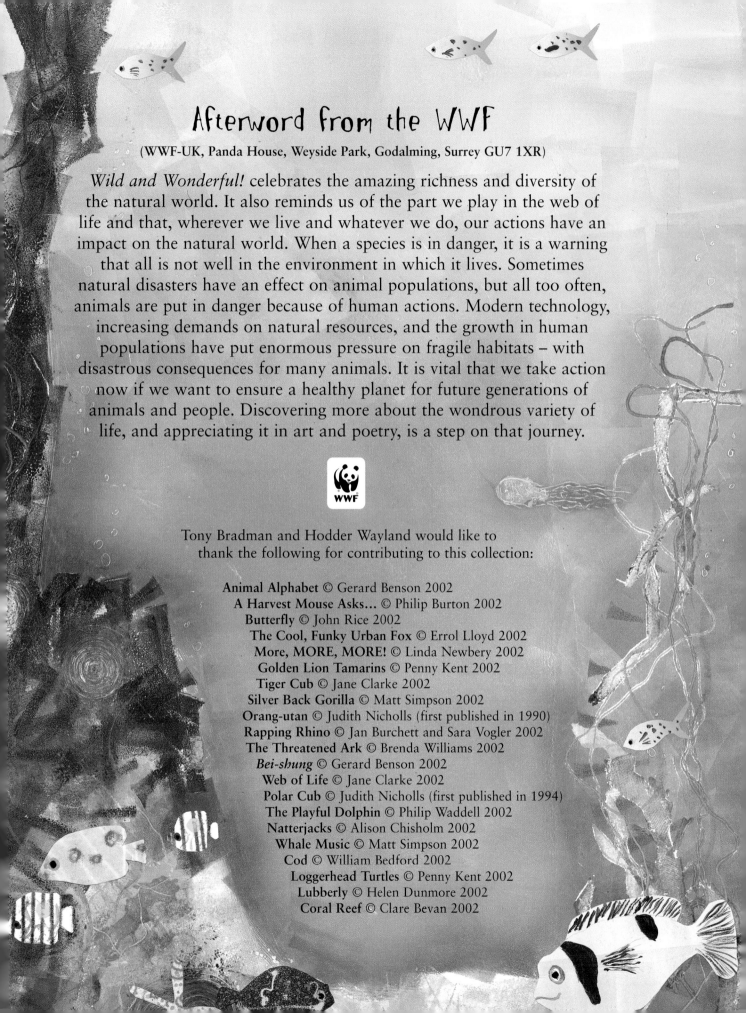

WWF

Tony Bradman and Hodder Wayland would like to thank the following for contributing to this collection:

Animal Alphabet © Gerard Benson 2002
A Harvest Mouse Asks… © Philip Burton 2002
Butterfly © John Rice 2002
The Cool, Funky Urban Fox © Errol Lloyd 2002
More, MORE, MORE! © Linda Newbery 2002
Golden Lion Tamarins © Penny Kent 2002
Tiger Cub © Jane Clarke 2002
Silver Back Gorilla © Matt Simpson 2002
Orang-utan © Judith Nicholls (first published in 1990)
Rapping Rhino © Jan Burchett and Sara Vogler 2002
The Threatened Ark © Brenda Williams 2002
Bei-shung © Gerard Benson 2002
Web of Life © Jane Clarke 2002
Polar Cub © Judith Nicholls (first published in 1994)
The Playful Dolphin © Philip Waddell 2002
Natterjacks © Alison Chisholm 2002
Whale Music © Matt Simpson 2002
Cod © William Bedford 2002
Loggerhead Turtles © Penny Kent 2002
Lubberly © Helen Dunmore 2002
Coral Reef © Clare Bevan 2002